Ideas Box!

Rainforests

Let's find out about the rainforest!

Deborah Chancellor

W
FRANKLIN WATTS
LONDON•SYDNEY

espresso
education

This edition 2013

Franklin Watts
338 Euston Road
London NW1 3BH

Franklin Watts Australia
Level 17/207 Kent Street
Sydney, NSW 2000

Text and illustration © Franklin Watts 2011

The Espresso characters are originated
and designed by Claire Underwood and
Pesky Ltd.

The Espresso characters are the property
of Espresso Education Ltd.

A CIP catalogue record for this book is
available from the British Library.

ISBN: 978 1 4451 0402 7
Dewey: 333.7'5

Series Editor: Sarah Peutrill
Art Director: Jonathan Hair
Designer: Matt Lilly
Illustrations: Artful Doodlers
Picture Researcher: Diana Morris

Every attempt has been made to clear
copyright. Should there be any inadvertent
omission please apply to the publisher
for rectification.

Printed in China

Franklin Watts is a division of Hachette
Children's Books, an Hachette UK company.
www.hachette.co.uk

PIcture credits:
Eugene Berman/Shutterstock: 5t. Dan
Brandenburg/istockphoto: 26b. Michael
Branstetter/antweb.org: 10b. Alieisha
Evans/Shutterstock: 17tr. Scott Garrett/
istockphoto: 16bl. greglith/Shutterstock:
14br. Tom Grill/istockphoto: 13br.
Guentermanaus/Shutterstock: 6t. Martin
Harvey/NHPA: 23c. Inoman/istockphoto:
24c. Rafa Irusta/Shutterstock: 7t. Eric
Isselée/istockphoto: 17br. Jaggat/
Shutterstock: 24b. Tamara Kulikova/
Shutterstock: 5c inset. Reistlin Magere/
Shutterstock: 5tcb. Bob Masters /Alamy:
23t. Neil McAllister/Alamy: 8bl.
Christopher Meder/Shutterstock: 5tc inset.
Gleison Miranda/ Funai/AP/PAI: 22b.
Marcin Niemiec/Shutterstock: 5b. Edward
Parker/Alamy: 29b. Jaana Piira/
Shutterstock: 5tc. Heinz Plange/Alamy: 5tcb
inset. Prill Mediendesign & Fotografie/
istockphoto: 7b, 19tr. Johan.R/Shutterstock:
9b. Luiz Claudio Ribeiro/Shutterstock: 5tr
inset. Roberto A Sanchez/istockphoto: 17c.
Marcel Schauer/Shutterstock: 1, 18c.
Jurgen & Christine Sohns/FLPA: 12b.
Paul Springett/Alamy: 28t.T-Immagini/
istockphoto: 16c. Dave Watts/Alamy: 11c. S
Zefel/Shutterstock: 5c.

Contents

 Pages with this symbol have a downloadable photocopiable sheet (see page 30).

What is a rainforest?

Sal's Auntie Lizzy is about to go on an exciting adventure holiday. She is travelling to the Amazon rainforest to see some of the amazing animals and plants that live there. Sal and Ash are looking at a map of South America, to see where Auntie Lizzy is going.

Amazon rainforest

SOUTH AMERICA

Wow! The Amazon rainforest is HUGE!

Fast facts

- Rainforests have been around for 400 million years.
- There are two different kinds of rainforest: tropical and temperate.
- Temperate rainforests are cool and wet, and are found in mild climates near the coast.
- Tropical rainforests are hot and wet, and are found near the equator.
- The Amazon rainforest is a tropical rainforest.
- Rainforests only cover 6% of the Earth's surface.
- Over half of the world's plant and animal species live in rainforests.
- Rainforests are home to over 80% of all the world's insects.

Ash finds some pictures of a tropical rainforest. They show the different layers of the rainforest and some animals that live there, from the dark forest floor, up through the leafy canopy to the towering treetops.

TROPICAL RAINFOREST

Emergent layer

Harpy eagle

Howler monkey

Canopy

Anaconda

Understorey

I wish I could climb like a monkey.

Tapir

Forest floor

Science spot: adaptation

Rainforest animals are perfectly suited, or adapted, to their habitat. Toucans live in the Amazon rainforest. They have huge beaks, which they use to crack open nuts. With two claws in the front and two in the back of each foot, they can balance on branches.

Rainforests around the world

Sal's Auntie Lizzie has arrived in the Amazon rainforest. She sent Sal a postcard, to tell her all about it.

Dear Sal,

I'm here at last! I went on a boat trip down the Amazon River today, and saw some awesome animals. A huge lizard called a green iguana fell off a branch into the water as we passed by...

I spotted a capybara on the riverbank – it's the world's biggest rodent. It looked just like your pet guinea pig, but it was the size of a goat!

Love from Auntie Lizzy xxxxx

Quiz:
The Amazon is the world's biggest rainforest. How big is it?

A) Almost as big as Australia

B) The size of London

C) As big as the UK

Quiz answers are on page 32.

English spot: write a postcard

Imagine that you are travelling in the rainforest like Polly's aunt. Think about all the animals and plants you might see. Write a postcard home to tell your family about your rainforest trip.

North America

Europe

Asia

Africa

Equator

South America

Australasia

This world map shows where rainforests grow. Tropical rainforests are shown in dark green, and temperate rainforests in light green.

Fast facts

- Tropical rainforests are found in every continent except Europe and Antarctica.
- Temperate rainforests grow in parts of North and South America, Australasia and Europe.
- In tropical rainforests, it is usually as hot as 25°C and it rains most days.
- Temperate rainforests have two seasons – a long, rainy season, and a shorter, foggy one.
- Both tropical and temperate rainforests usually have over 200 centimetres of rain a year.

Every year, at least 250 centimetres of rain falls in the African rainforest. In the UK it only rains about 93 centimetres a year.

Rainforest river

Sal decides to write a poem about a river in a rainforest. She tries to imagine what a rainforest river is really like, and writes a list of sights, sounds, smells and sensations. She finds out about the animals that live there. She makes the poem's shape like a river.

Can you write a river poem like me?

Sliding smoothly past, not too slow or fast, sunlight flashes, raindrop splashes, nighttime falls at last.

Sal discovers that people in rainforests use rivers for food, water and transport. Rivers in rainforests flood in the rainy season. In parts of Southeast Asia, rainforest people live in stilt houses, so they are not affected by the floods. Kim thinks this would be fun, because he likes walking on stilts.

Fast facts

- The Amazon River is the world's widest river.
- The Amazon River is 6,400 kilometres long. It is the second longest river in the world, after the Nile.
- The Amazon River flows through five countries: Brazil, Peru, Bolivia, Colombia and Ecuador.
- About a quarter of all the world's freshwater is in the Amazon River.
- More freshwater fish live in the Amazon River than anywhere else on Earth.

Quiz:
How wide is the Amazon River?

A) 120-200 metres wide

B) 6-10 kilometres wide

C) 60-100 kilometres wide

The piranha swims in the Amazon River. A shoal of hungry piranha can strip a large animal to its bones in just a few minutes with their razor-sharp teeth.

River wide and deep, what secrets do you keep? Brown as bark, cool and dark, you never stop to sleep.

Life on the forest floor

Ash wants to find out more about the rainforest floor. It is a dark place – not much light passes through the leaves to reach the ground. But it is an exciting place of discovery. Scientists are still finding new species there. Ash reads about a newly-discovered species of ant. He writes a report about it.

 ········· Espresso Extra ·········

Our reporter, Ash, investigates a brand new species.

ANT FROM MARS!

A brand new species of ant has been discovered in the Amazon rainforest. It is nicknamed 'the ant from Mars', because it looks like it comes from another planet!

0.5 mm

Martialis heureka – the ant from Mars.

What's new?

The ant lives under the leafy forest floor. It is totally blind and has big jaws, which it probably uses to catch its prey. Scientists believe that ants like this have been around for about 120 million years, since the time of the dinosaurs.

By Ash

Science spot: biodiversity

Biodiversity is the variety of living things in a particular place. Can you count the number of different plants and wild animals in your school garden? You may need some help with this! Of all the different habitats on Earth, rainforests have the biggest variety of creatures and plants. It is one of the many reasons why the rainforests must be protected. If they disappear, biodiversity is threatened.

When a rainforest is cut down, animals lose their natural habitat and may become extinct.

The Australian rainforest is now so small that there are only about 1,500 wild Southern Cassowaries (pictured) left roaming about on the forest floor.

Quiz:
Where are the shortest rainforest plants?

A) In the rainforest canopy

B) In the rainforest river

C) On the forest floor

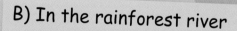

Up in the trees

Kim and Eddy see a programme about rainforest animals that live high up in the trees. They love seeing how monkeys and apes move from branch to branch. Eddy thinks sloths are funny. They hang upside down in trees, and are much slower than monkeys. It takes them a minute to move about three metres.

I can swing like a monkey.

I can hang like a sloth.

Sal gets another postcard from her Auntie Lizzie. She shows it to Kim and Eddy.

Dear Sal,
Guess what, I've been exploring in the rainforest! Yesterday I saw a black spider monkey swing through the canopy – he gripped the branches with his tail. How cool was that? I'm flying home tomorrow, so see you soon.
Love from
Auntie Lizzy xxxxx

PE spot: movement

Watch the way that rainforest animals move. Visit a zoo to see the animals for yourself. Gorillas, chimpanzees and forest elephants live in the African rainforest. Frogs, snakes and crocodiles live in the Australian rainforest. Try to copy how these animals move. Can your friends guess which animal you are pretending to be?

Quiz:
Where is most animal life found in a rainforest?

A) Up in the canopy among the trees

B) On the forest floor

C) In the rainforest river

Californian redwoods grow up to 115 metres tall – that's as tall as 20 giraffes!

Rainforest trees are just as amazing as the animals that live in them. The world's tallest trees grow in temperate rainforests.

Play the music of the rainforest

Sal, Polly and Ash try to find out about rainforest sounds and the noises the rainforest animals make to communicate. In the Amazon rainforest, red howler monkeys can be heard five kilometres away! The three friends listen to rainforest animals, to help them compose some music. They perform their music with percussion instruments.

You will need:

- Books, websites and videos about rainforest animals
- Percussion instruments, eg xylophone, clave, two-tone woodblock, cabasa, bongo drums, castanets
- Cassette player or video camera to record your music

1 Find out about some rainforest animals. Choose a variety of animals, for example slow, fast, big, small, loud and quiet ones.

Xylophone

Two-tone woodblock

Bongo drums

Science spot: musical food chain

A food chain shows who eats who in a particular habitat. Think about the animals you have described in your music (below). You could put the different musical pieces in order of who eats who, ending up with the biggest hunter. For example, music about a fish could be followed by music about a crocodile, then an anaconda.

2 Watch videos of your animals and listen to the noises they make. Some animal websites have recordings of animal sounds. Choose instruments that will suit your animals, such as cabasa for snakes, castanets for insects.

3 Try out different rhythms and sound patterns. Match the speed, rhythm and volume with your animals.

4 Don't forget to record your results! Play your music back when you have finished.

Cabasa

Castanets

Clave

Colourful rainforests

Sal and Polly discover that some rainforest animals use colour to help them blend in with their surroundings. This is called camouflage. Sal and Polly experiment with camouflage. They paint each other's faces like rainforest animals.

Let's play hide and seek in the woods!

Stick insects are almost impossible to spot on the branch of a rainforest tree. This helps them hide from their enemies. Sal finds out that other rainforest animals use colour to help them creep up on prey. For example, the jaguar's spotted coat helps it disappear into the leafy shadows.

A jaguar camouflaged on the forest floor.

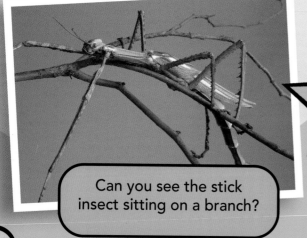

Can you see the stick insect sitting on a branch?

?

Feedback...

Do you think camouflage is more useful for hunters or for their prey? Why?

Art connections: patterns

Rainforest insects often display beautiful patterns and colours. Look at the wings of some rainforest butterflies, for example the Postman butterfly from South America, and the Birdwing butterfly from Australia. Have a go at copying these colours and patterns. You could make a potato print. Ask an adult to help you cut a shape into a potato. Dip the shape into paint and make prints onto paper.

Postman

Birdwing

I printed some butterflies to make wrapping paper for a present.

Some rainforest animals are brightly coloured to warn hunters away. They may be poisonous, or just copying the colours of another poisonous animal.

The brilliant colours of the poison dart frog of the Amazon warn other animals that it has toxic skin.

Animals in danger

The orang-utan is Kim's favourite rainforest animal. He is worried because the orang-utan is in danger of becoming extinct. He makes a poster to put up at school to tell his friends about the problem.

The orang-utan needs your help!

SAVE THE ORANG-UTAN

- The orang-utan is a kind of ape. It is one of our closest animal relatives.

- Orang-utans live in rainforests in Southeast Asia.

- In the last 20 years, over 80 per cent of the orang-utans' rainforest home has been destroyed.

- There are only about 50,000 orang-utans left in the wild.

Adopt an orang-utan: go to the Worldwide Fund for Nature website: www.wwf.org.uk/adoption/orangutan

Many rainforest animals are endangered, because their habitat is disappearing. These animals are perfectly adapted to the rainforest, and can't survive easily anywhere else. Sadly, when an animal becomes extinct, it can never be replaced.

Endangered rainforest animals
- SOUTH AMERICA
  Giant otter, Golden lion tamarin, Three-toed sloth
- AFRICA
  Mountain gorilla, Eastern red colobus, Chimpanzee
- SOUTHEAST ASIA
  Sumatran tiger, Asian elephant, Javan rhinoceros
- AUSTRALIA
  Southern cassowary, Sharman's rock wallaby, Spotted tailed quoll

I think all animals are important and we should try to help endangered animals.

Geography spot: conservation

In the African rainforest, conservation work to protect the mountain gorilla is helping this rare, gentle giant. Find out about endangered rainforest animals around the world, and projects to save them. Get a world map, and stick on photos of endangered rainforest animals in the places where they live.

?

Feedback...

Do you think it really matters if species become extinct?

Make a rainforest game

Ash, Sal, Kim and Polly have invented a rainforest card game. They found out about rainforest animals to make the game. They discovered which rainforest animals are hunters, and which ones are prey. Then they used this information to make and play the game.

You will need:

- Books and websites on rainforest animals
- Sheet of card (50x30cm)
- Pens and pencils
- Ruler
- Scissors

2 Mark the edges of your card at intervals of 5cm. Draw a grid on the card, linking the marks on each side. You should have 60 squares, each one measuring 5x5cm. Cut out the squares to make 60 cards.

1 Make a list of six animals that hunt in the rainforest, such as jaguar, piranha, anaconda, tiger, crocodile and eagle. Make a list of 12 animals that are hunted in the rainforest — this list can include fish, insects, small birds, frogs, small monkeys and other small mammals.

Crocodile

Piranha

Tiger

Anaconda

Jaguar

Eagle

3 Draw and label each hunter on two cards. You should have 12 'hunter' cards in total. Draw and label each hunted animal on four cards. You should have 48 'hunted' cards.

I'm the King of the Jungle!

4 Shuffle the cards, and deal them out to four players. You should have 15 cards each. Place the cards face down. Take it in turns to play a card, face up so everyone can see. The person with the hunter card wins the set. If a set has more than one hunter, or all the cards are hunted animals, then decide which animal is strongest. When all the cards have been played, the winner has the most cards.

Play more games

Use your rainforest cards to play other games that you know, such as snap or pairs. Try inventing a new game.

People of the rainforest

Ash wants to know who lives in the Amazon rainforest. He discovers that people have lived there for 15,000 years. Five hundred years ago, there were ten million Amazonian Indians. Many died when explorers arrived from Europe. Today, there are only about 200,000 Amazonian Indians left. They live in over 200 different tribes and speak 180 languages.

Ash finds out about a tribe that has just been discovered in the Amazon. He writes a newspaper report.

Espresso Extra

 Our reporter, Ash, investigates an un-contacted tribe.

FIRST CONTACT

A tribe has been seen for the first time, deep in the Amazon rainforest. In 2008, photos were taken from the air, showing people from this tribe, and the place where they live.

In danger
Experts believe that around the world, there are over 100 undiscovered tribes like this one. Over half of them live in the Amazon. They are in danger, because their rainforest home is being destroyed.

By Ash

Rainforest people respect and care for their environment. They farm the forest without harming it, using its many fruits and plants for food and medicine. They only kill what they need for food and clothing.

Science spot: medicine

For centuries, rainforest people have used plants as medicine. Look on the Internet to find out about rainforest medicines. Over a quarter of all our medicines come from rainforest plants. For example, anti-cancer drugs have been made from the rosy periwinkle (left), a flower from the rainforests of Madagascar. However, the periwinkle is endangered just like many animals (see pages 18–19).

The Yanomami is one of the biggest tribes in the Amazon. They are known for face painting and body piercing.

Rainforest plants can be very good for you!

? Feedback...

Do you think we can learn anything from rainforest people?

Disappearing rainforests

Ash tells Polly that over the last 50 years, more rainforests have been cut down than ever before. Polly can't understand why rainforests are being destroyed, if they are home to so many living things. Ash explains that rainforests are often cleared to make way for cattle ranches and soya fields.

A lot of the beef and soya we eat comes from rainforest areas.

This area of rainforest has been cleared to make room for a cattle ranch.

Fast facts

- Rainforests in Southeast Asia are cut down to make way for palm oil plantations.
- Rainforests are destroyed to make way for cattle farms and soya bean plantations.
- More than half of the world's rainforests have now disappeared.
- As rainforests disappear, it is estimated that about 137 species of animals and plants are lost every day.
- More species are becoming extinct today than at any other time since the dinosaurs.

This palm oil plantation is on rainforest land in Thailand.

Rainforests are important for the environment. Trees absorb, or take in, a gas in the air called carbon dioxide. This gas traps the Sun's heat close to the Earth, making the world warmer. If the rainforests disappear, there will be more carbon dioxide in the atmosphere. Temperatures will rise, and climates will change.

Sun

Carbon dioxide, and other greenhouse gases, trap some of the Sun's heat.

Rising temperatures have changed some of the weather patterns around the world.

Atmosphere

Rainforest destruction adds to the problem of global warming.

Science spot: climate change

Climates are slowly changing because of global warming. In the future, some parts of the world will get more rain, and others will get less. The destruction of the rainforests is one cause of climate change, but there are others. Find out what they are. There are two clues on the diagram above.

Quiz:

If we keep destroying the rainforests at the same rate, how long will it take for them to disappear?

A) 5 years

B) 100 years

C) 40 years

Save the rainforest!

The Espresso friends want to do something to save the rainforest. Polly has a good idea. She suggests they make some crafts to sell. Sal shows them how to make clay pots in the shape of rainforest animals. They give the money they raise to a conservation charity, to help protect rainforests around the world.

My pot looks like a frog.

Art spot: pottery

Pots made from clay, stone and wood have been found in many parts of the Amazon rainforest. They were made by Amazonian Indians, and some are hundreds of years old. Many are shaped like animals, or decorated with pictures of them.

This pot was made in the Amazon rainforest.

The friends are very careful about what they buy, so they can help to save rainforests around the world. They try to find out where their food comes from, so they don't eat anything that was farmed on rainforest land. They ask their families not to buy wooden furniture made from precious rainforest trees, such as teak and mahogany.

Many shampoos and soaps contain palm oil. Find out if the oil is from a plantation on rainforest land.

Check to make sure the beef or soya that you eat doesn't come from rainforest lands.

Check the wood you buy is from a forest where trees are planted, as well as cut down. This is called sustainable wood.

Buy fruit and nuts grown on rainforest trees, to stop new crops being farmed on rainforest land.

Have a rainforest debate

Ash, Kim, Sal and Polly are having a debate about ecotourism. This is when people go on special holidays that try to help protect natural areas. Sal and Ash think ecotourism is a great idea, but Polly and Kim are not sure.

Ecotourists visit undeveloped parts of the world to find out about the people, animals and plants that live there.

My auntie had a fantastic holiday in the Amazon.

Can she take me next time?

Sal and Ash think ecotourists have amazing adventures, and learn a lot at the same time. Money from ecotourism is used to fund conservation projects.

Polly and Kim think ecotourism damages the environment and disturbs rare animals. It also interrupts and changes the lives of local people.

Don't disturb rare animals!

We should leave rainforest people alone.

Drama spot: hot seating

Dams are built across rivers in rainforests to make electricity.

- Environmental campaigners think dams are expensive and harm the rainforest.
- Conservationists think dams endanger some rainforest animals and habitats.
- Politicians think dams provide useful hydro-electric power for towns and cities.
- Rainforest people think dams destroy their traditional way of life.

Imagine you belong to one of these groups of people, and argue their case with your friends. You are in the 'hot seat' – answer questions from this person's point of view. Try the activity again, taking another person's argument.

People disagree about whether it is a good or bad idea to build dams across rivers in rainforests.

Glossary

adapted The way an animal is suited to its habitat.

atmosphere A layer of gases around the Earth.

biodiversity The variety of living things in a place.

camouflage How an animal blends with its background to avoid being seen.

canopy At tree level in a rainforest.

climate The pattern of weather in a place over a period of time.

conservation Looking after the environment.

continent One of the Earth's main land masses.

ecotourism A kind of holiday that teaches people about the environment.

emergent layer The highest layer of a rainforest, above the canopy.

endangered In danger of dying out.

environment The world around us, and everything in it.

equator An imaginary line around the middle of the Earth.

extinct Died out, no longer existing.

forest floor The lowest level of a rainforest.

global warming An increase in temperatures around the world.

greenhouse gases Any of the gases in the Earth's atmosphere that contribute to global warming.

habitat The place where an animal or plant lives.

hydro-electric power Electricity made from the power of moving water.

plantation A large farm where crops are grown.

prey An animal that is hunted by another animal.

shoal A group of fish swimming together.

species A group of animals or plants that differ in only small ways.

sustainable Way of life where human needs are met without reducing the ability of other people, wild species or people in future to survive.

temperate From a mild climate.

toxic Poisonous.

tropical From a hot, wet climate.

tribe A group of people who live together.

understorey Plants that grow at a low level in a rainforest.

Activity sheets

Go to www.franklinwatts.co.uk/downloads for free activity sheets.
Page 5: Design your own rainforest animal to show how it is adapted to its particular habitat.
Page 7: Find out about endangered animals and draw them on a world map.
Page 20: Some templates for the rainforest card game.

Espresso connections

Here are a few ideas for how to take the contents of this book further using Espresso. There are many more resources on rainforests listed in the staffroom area under 'Resource Boxes'.

What is a rainforest? (pages 4–5)
Find out more about rainforests in *Geography 2 > WWW > Environmental issues*. Learn about animal adaptations in *Science 2 > Habitats (further resources)* and design an animal in the *Activities* section.

Rainforests around the world (pages 6–7)
To find useful map resources, go to *Geography 2 > WWW > Maps and globes*. For a template for writing a postcard, visit *Geography 1 > Passport > Brazil*.

Rainforest river (pages 8–9)
For examples of river poetry, go to *English 2 > Further resources > River poetry*. To watch a video about swimming in the Amazon, look at *Geography 2 > News archive > Rivers*.

Life on the forest floor (pages 10–11)
To read more about animal and plant discoveries in rainforests, read the article 'New plants and animals discovered' in *Science 2 > News archive > Animals > Animals from around the world*. For further information about the cassowary, look at *Science 2 > News archive > Animals > Endangered species > Australian cassowary bird threatened with extinction*.

Up in the trees (pages 12–13)
Watch a video on rainforest animal movements in *Foundation > Creative > Animal moves*. Learn about measuring animals in *Maths 2 > Measures > Length*.

Play the music of the rainforest (pages 14–15)
For help and information about composing music, look at the resources in the Music search (Level 1 & 2) in *Music 2 (voices of the lion: tropical sounds)* and take the *Exploring musical composition* Learning path.

Colourful rainforests (pages 16–17)
To watch videos and find out more about camouflage, go to *Science 2 > Habitats > Activities > Animal adaptations*.

Animals in danger (pages 18–19)
For a video about endangered mountain gorillas, go to *Geography 2 > Going Green Resource box (Wild world > Video vault)*. To find out more about endangered animals, take a look in *Science 2 > News Archive > Animals*.

Make a rainforest game (pages 20–21)
Watch a video about animal diets in *Science 1 > Animal life (eating)*. To find out more about food chains, look at *Science 2 > Habitats > Activities*.

People of the rainforest (pages 22–23)
For help with writing a news report, go to *English 2 > Further resources > News Bites (create your own news report)* and the *News Resource box*. For news reports about rainforest communities, visit *Geography 2 > News archive > People around the world* and *Geography 2 > News archive > Environmental issues > Rainforest* for news about threats to rainforests.

Disappearing rainforests (pages 24–25)
To learn more about climate change, look at articles and videos in *Geography 2 > News archive > Environmental issues > Climate change* and *Geography 2 > News archive > Environmental issues > Rainforest*.

Save the rainforest! (pages 26–27)
To see pictures of Amazonian clay pots, visit *Art 2 > News archive > Sculpture > Amazonian art exhibition*. For further resources on saving the rainforest, go to *Geography 2 > Passport > Madagascar* and in *Science 2 > News archive > Plants > Saving the rainforests: (parts 1 and 2)*.

Have a rainforest debate (pages 28–29)
For help in organising a hot-seating exercise, go to *English 2 > Speaking and Listening gallery > Interviewing*. To practise deciding between facts and opinion in a debate, go to *English 2 > Activities and Learning Tools > Fact or opinion*.

Index

Quiz answers

Page 6: A) Almost as big as Australia

Page 9: B) During the dry season, the Amazon River is 6–10 km wide. (During the wet season it is around 48 km wide.)

Page 11: C) The shortest rainforest plants grow on the forest floor, where there isn't much light.

Page 13: A) Over half of all rainforest animals live up in the trees in the canopy.

Page 25: C) Our rainforests could disappear in under 40 years.